WHERE IS MY COUNTRY?

by Robin Nelson

first step nonfiction

Lerner Publications Company · Minneapolis

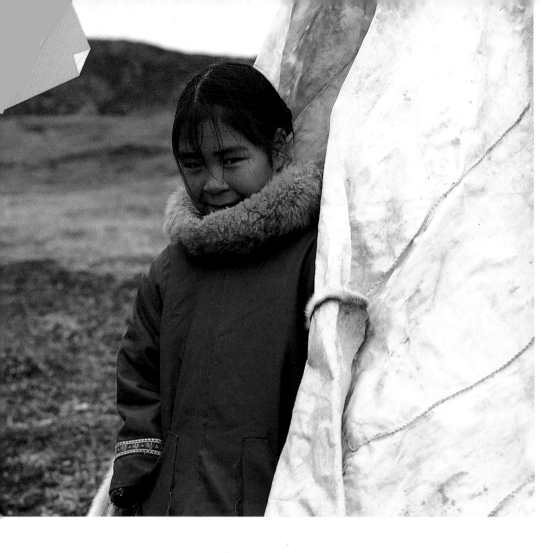

I live in a **country**.

A country can have many
cities and **towns**.

A country can be very big.

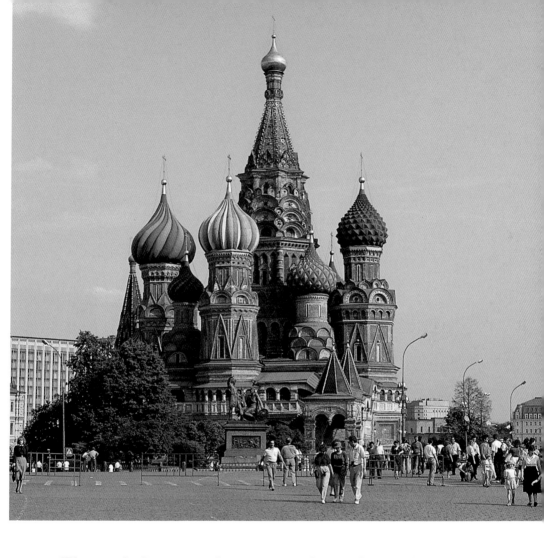

The biggest country is bigger than most **continents**.

Vatican City

A country can be very small.

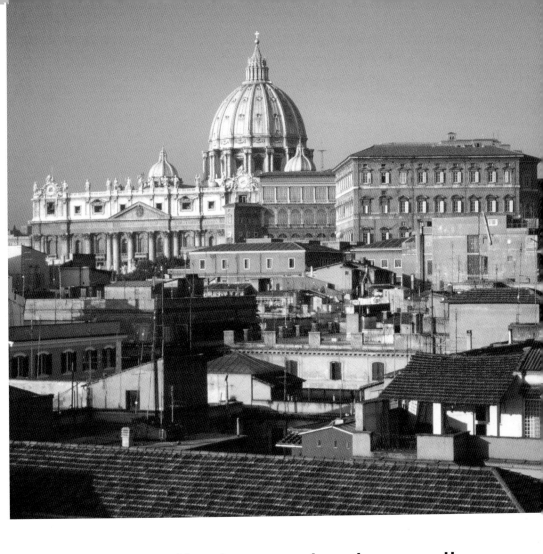

The smallest country is smaller than most cities.

My country is the United States of America.

Most of my country is on the continent of North America.

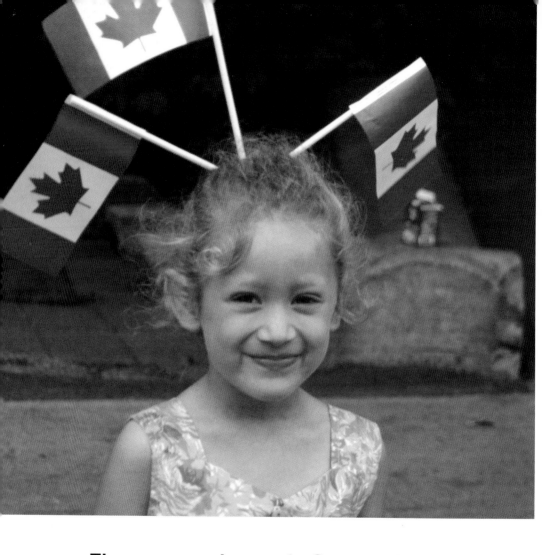

The country of Canada is
north of my country.

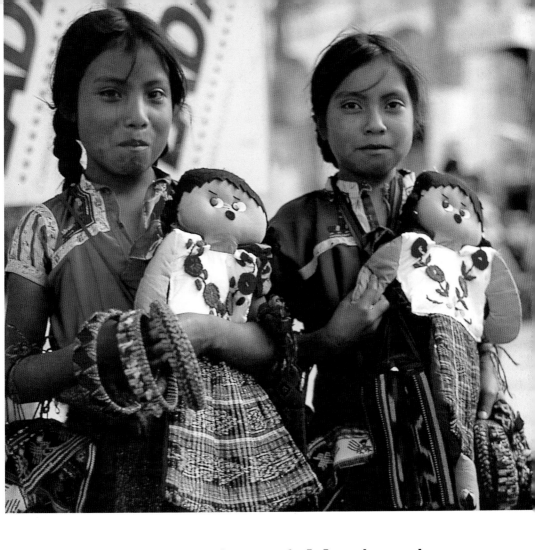

The country of Mexico is
south of my country.

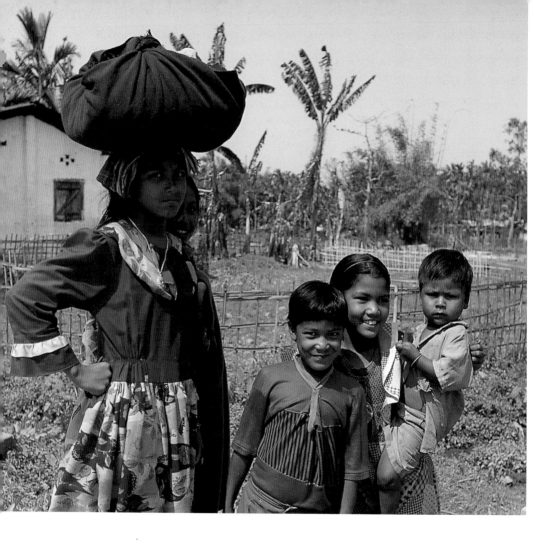

There are families living in countries all over the world.

Some countries have land on all sides.

Some countries are by the
ocean.

Some countries are by the mountains.

Where is my country?

My country is on my continent,
where I live with my family.

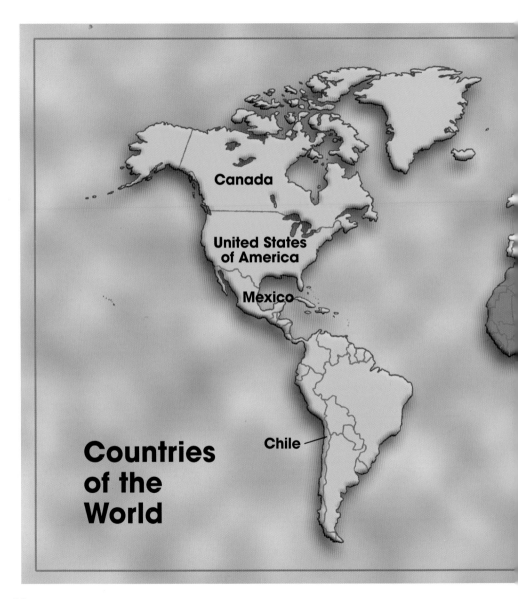

Canada

United States
of America

Mexico

Chile

**Countries
of the
World**

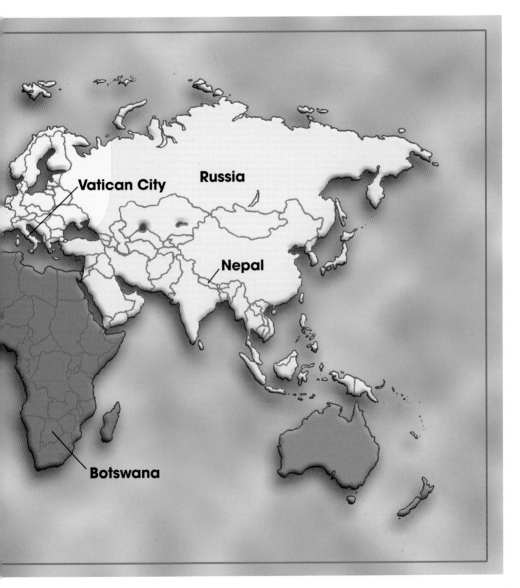

Vatican City

Russia

Nepal

Botswana

Country Facts

The world's smallest country is Vatican City. It is located within another country—Italy.

The biggest country is Russia. Russia stretches across two continents—Asia and Europe.

The United States is the third largest country in the world in population after China and India.

Australia is the only country that is also a continent.

The United States is divided into 7 regions:
1. New England
2. Middle Atlantic States
3. Southern States
4. Midwestern States
5. Rocky Mountain States
6. Southwestern States
7. Pacific Coast States

 The U.S. bird is the bald eagle.

 The U.S. flower is the rose.

Glossary

 cities – places where many people live and work. A city is a large town.

 continents – seven large land masses on the earth

 country – a place where people live and share the same laws

 towns – places where people live and work. A town is smaller than a city.

Index

The photographs in this book are reproduced through the courtesy of: © Earth Imaging/Stone, front cover, p. 9; © Wolfgang Kaehler, pp. 2, 3, 5, 12, 16, 22 (top and bottom); © John Heseltine/Corbis, p. 7; © Earl Kowall/Corbis, p. 10; © M. Bryan Ginsberg, p. 11; © Todd Powell/Photo Network, p. 17.

Lerner Publications Company
A division of Lerner Publishing Group
241 First Avenue North
Minneapolis, MN 55401 U.S.A.

Website address: www.lernerbooks.com

Library of Congress Cataloging-in-Publication Data

Nelson, Robin, 1971–
      Where is my country? / by Robin Nelson.
          p.   cm. — (First step nonfiction)
      Includes index.
      ISBN-13: 978–0–8225–0192–3 (lib. bdg. : alk. paper)
      ISBN-10: 0–8225–0192–9 (lib. bdg. : alk. paper)
      1. Geography—Juvenile literature. 2. Family—Juvenile literature. [1. Geography.]
      I. Title. II. Series.
      G133.N37 2002
      910—dc21   2001000962

Manufactured in the United States of America
5 6 7 8 9 10 – DP – 11 10 09 08 07 06